really easy piano

BILLY JOEL

ISBN 978-1-70516-728-1

Visit Hal Leonard Online at
www.halleonard.com

World headquarters, contact:
Hal Leonard
7777 West Bluemound Road
Milwaukee, WI 53213
Email: info@halleonard.com

In Europe, contact:
Hal Leonard Europe Limited
42 Wigmore Street
Marylebone, London, W1U 2RY
Email: info@halleonardeurope.com

In Australia, contact:
Hal Leonard Australia Pty. Ltd.
4 Lentara Court
Cheltenham, Victoria, 3192 Australia
Email: info@halleonard.com.au

BILLY JOEL

really easy piano

Honesty

Words and Music by Billy Joel

This was the third single released from Joel's 1979 album, *52nd Street*, named after the New York street central to the jazz scene in the '40s and '50s. Joel was inspired by The Beatles' *Abbey Road* album title, named after the recording studio used by the group. Whilst recording in those days, producer Phil Ramone discovered the key to a successful studio take with Joel and his band – Chinese takeaway and full bellies!

Hints & Tips: There's no key signature to worry about in this song, but there are some sharps and flats here and there. The left hand often moves in half-steps, e.g. around the bottom of the first page. The time signature tells you to play in 'two', but think of it in 'four' if that's easier. Keep it steady throughout.

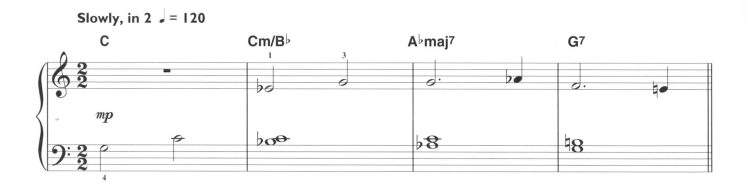

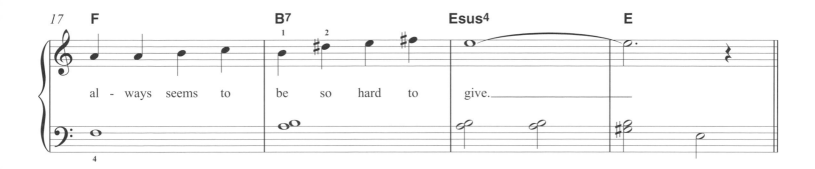

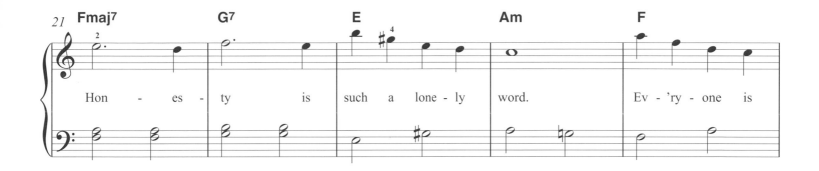

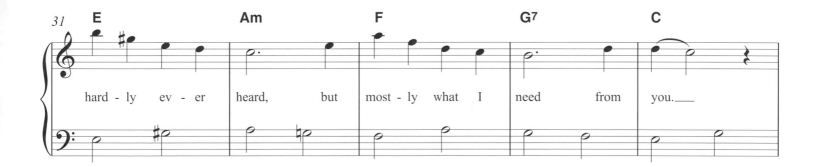

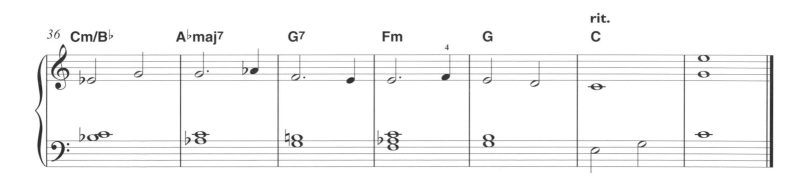

It's Still Rock and Roll to Me

Words and Music by Billy Joel

From his 1980 album, *Glass Houses*, here Joel expresses his dislike for music becoming more and more categorised in 'It's Still Rock and Roll to Me'. He addresses his critics in certain lines in the lyrics, reminding them that their opinion is not gospel to him! The song was a clear hit with his fans, achieving No. 1 on the Billboard Hot 100 for two weeks in July 1980. Joel would later go on to hit the US No. 1 spot again with 'Tell Her About It' and 'We Didn't Start the Fire'.

Hints & Tips: Take care with the 6/8 meter: you have to think in dotted crotchets/quarter notes and play with a swing. You could try it slower than the metronome marking at first; this will certainly help with all the sharps and flats you need to play, particularly on the last page.

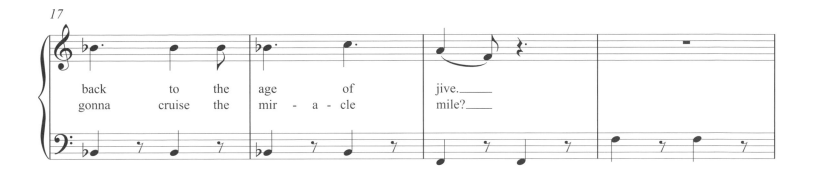

back to the age of jive.____
gonna cruise the mir - a - cle mile?____

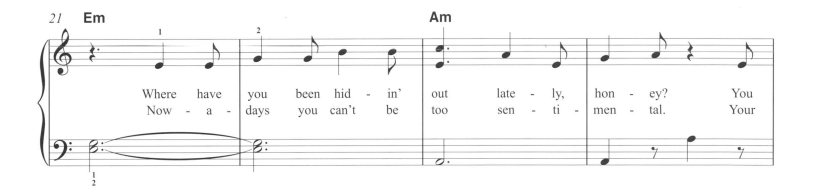

Em   **Am**

Where have you been hid - in' out late - ly, hon - ey? You
Now - a - days you can't be too sen - ti - men - tal. Your

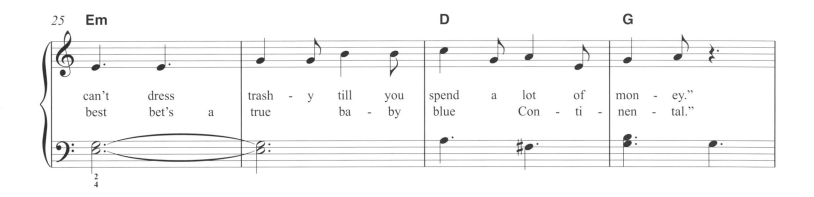

Em   **D**   **G**

can't dress trash - y till you spend a lot of mon - ey."
best bet's a true ba - by blue Con - ti - nen - tal."

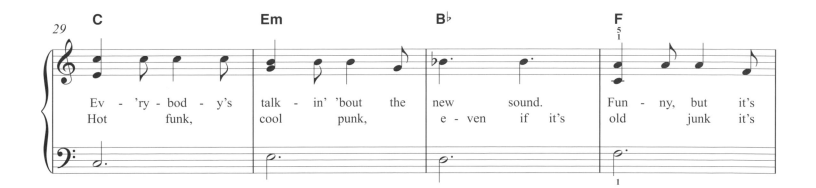

C   **Em**   **B♭**   **F**

Ev - 'ry - bod - y's talk - in' 'bout the new sound. Fun - ny, but it's
Hot funk, cool punk, e - ven if it's old junk it's

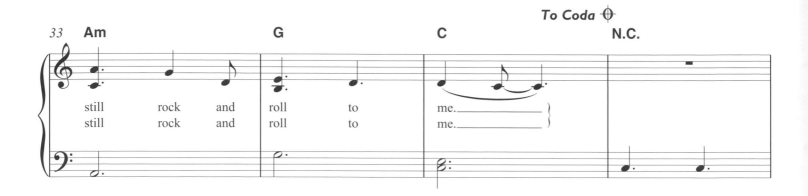

still rock and roll to me._____
still rock and roll to me._____

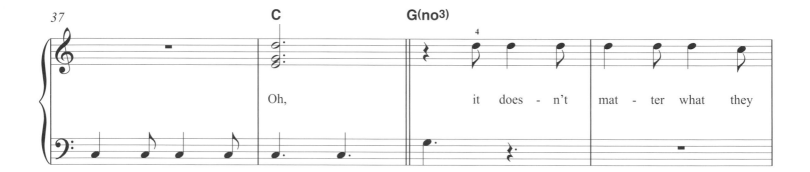

Oh, it does - n't mat - ter what they

say in the pa - pers, 'cause it's al - ways been the same old

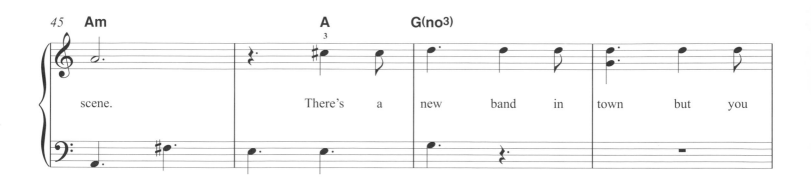

scene. There's a new band in town but you

can't get the sound from a sto - ry in a mag - a -

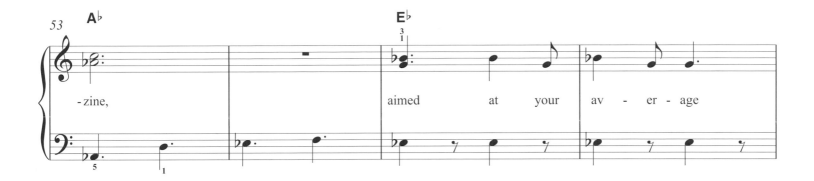

-zine, aimed at your av - er - age

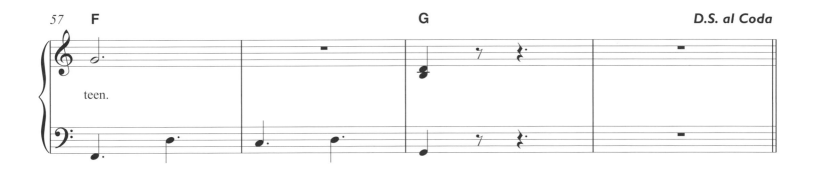

teen.

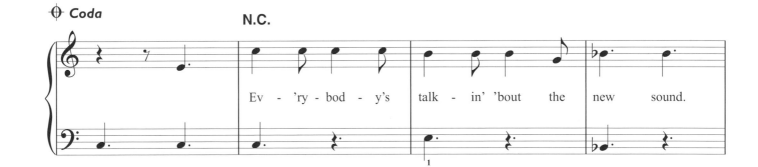

Coda

N.C.

Ev - 'ry - bod - y's talk - in' 'bout the new sound.

Fun - ny, but it's still rock and roll to me.

Just the Way You Are

Words and Music by Billy Joel

This song was written about Joel's first wife, Elizabeth, whom he met in his early twenties and married in 1973. The popular song almost didn't make it to an album, with Joel convinced it was too romantic, but after some persuasion from producer Phil Ramone, it became the first single release from his 1977 album, *The Stranger*. Joel split from Elizabeth after 9 years and has since gone on to marry three more times to Christie Brinkley in 1985, Katie Lee in 2004 and most recently, Alexis Roderick in 2015.

Hints & Tips: In this song, your hands really need to work together. The tune is passed from the right hand to the left in bar 10, and then back again. There are also places where you need to hold down two notes in one hand, like in the intro where the left hand holds the 'C' while also playing some harmony notes in the middle.

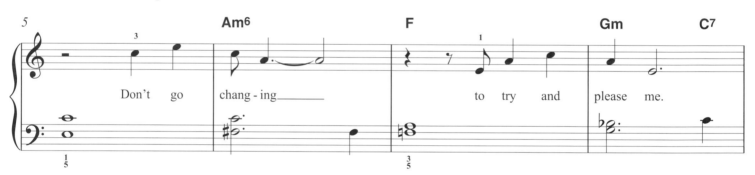

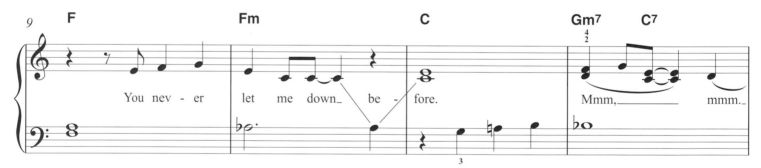

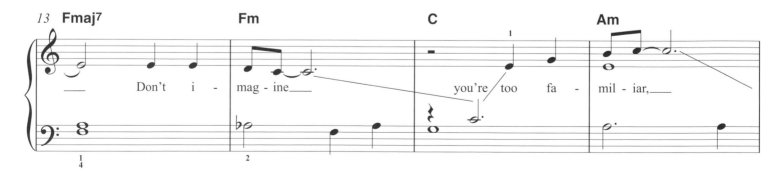

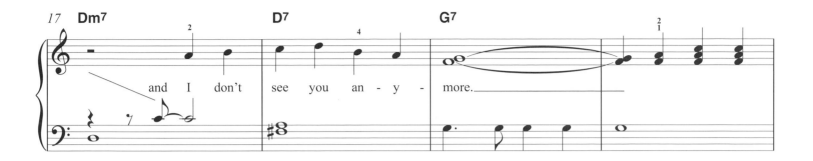

and I don't see you an-y - more._____

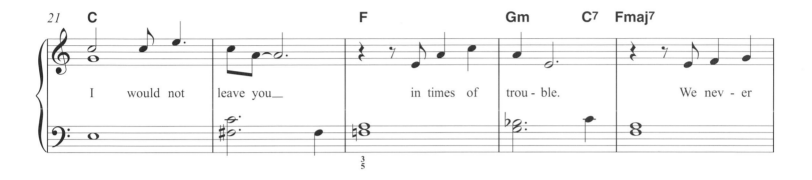

I would not leave you_____ in times of trou - ble. We nev - er

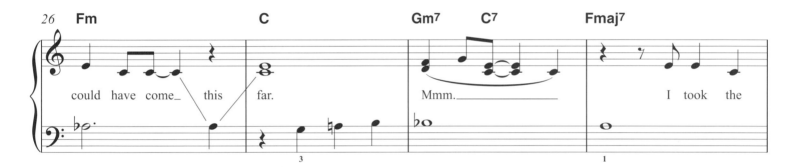

could have come__ this far. Mmm._____ I took the

good times,__ I'll take the bad times,__ I'll take you just the way you

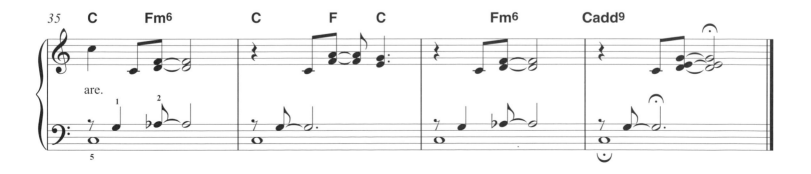

are.

The Longest Time

Words and Music by Billy Joel

This song was recorded almost completely 'a cappella', with the exception of a bass guitar as the only instrument accompanying Joel's many vocal tracks. From his 1983 album, *An Innocent Man*, Joel originally wanted this song performed with a vocal group, but due to availability issues, he ended up singing all the tracks himself. In order to avoid having the same vocal tone on every track, Joel invented characters for each part to vary his performances!

Hints & Tips: This song is in 2/2: two minims/half notes per bar, so it needs to feel like it's in 'two' rather than 'four'. At the same time, it shouldn't sound rushed; it should roll along in a relaxed style.

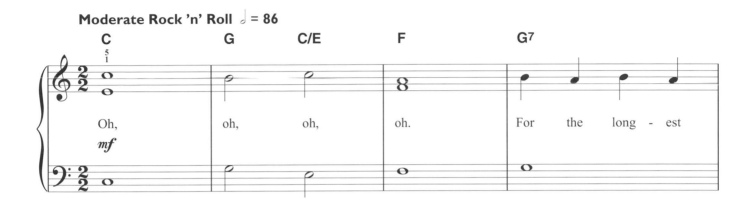

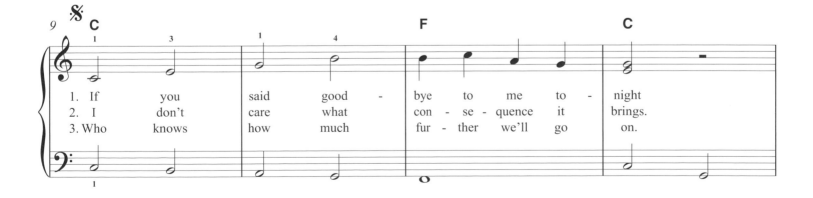

there would   still   be   mu - sic left to   write.
I   have   been   a   fool   for less - er things.
May - be   I'll be   sor - ry when you're gone.

What else could   I   do?   I'm so in - spired___ by you.
I want you   so   bad.   I   think you ought to know that
I'll take my   chanc - es.   I for - got how nice ro - mance is.

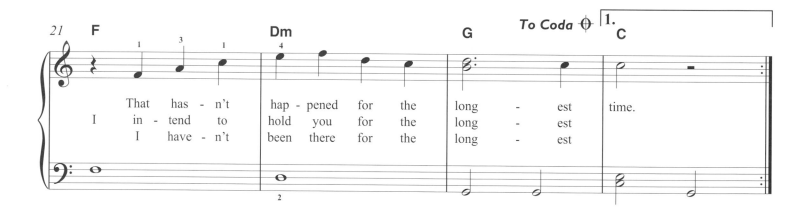

That has - n't hap - pened for the long - est   time.
I in - tend to hold you for the long - est
I have - n't been there for the long - est

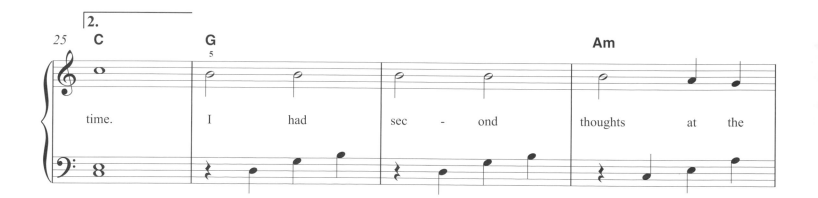

time.   I   had sec - ond   thoughts at the

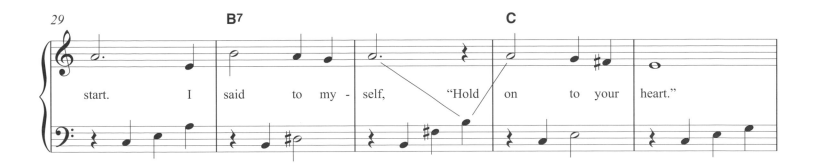

start. I said to my - self, "Hold on to your heart."

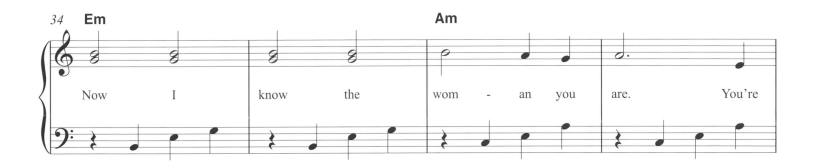

Now I know the wom - an you are. You're

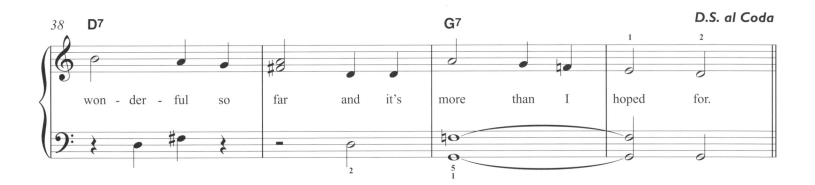

won - der - ful so far and it's more than I hoped for.

D.S. al Coda

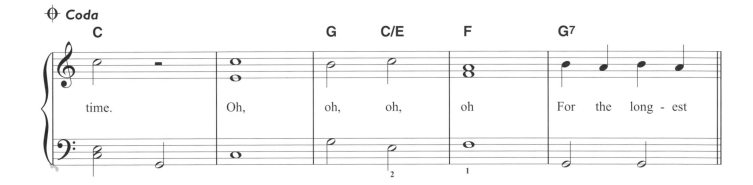

time. Oh, oh, oh, oh For the long - est

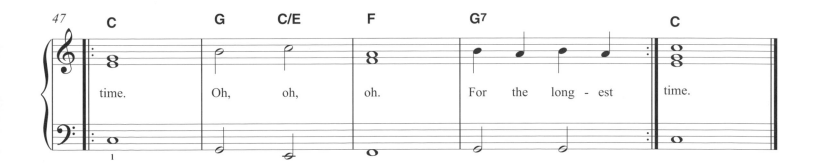

time. Oh, oh, oh. For the long - est time.

Movin' Out
(Anthony's Song)

Words and Music by Billy Joel

Movin' Out was the title of the 2002 Broadway stage production based on Joel's songs. The show closed in 2005 but continued to tour until 2007, with Joel winning a Tony award for the production's orchestration. Joel actually turned down the opportunity to work with George Martin, producer for The Beatles, on this record! Martin wanted to use a different band but Joel refused, instead turning to Phil Ramone who then became Joel's mentor and regular producer.

Hints & Tips: Keep this steady, as there are many repeated quavers/eighth notes in the right hand. Make sure you've got the B♭ in the key signature. There are also some other accidentals that crop up during the song.

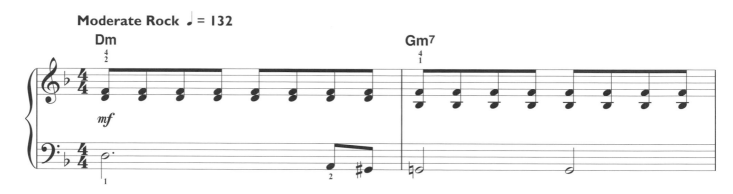

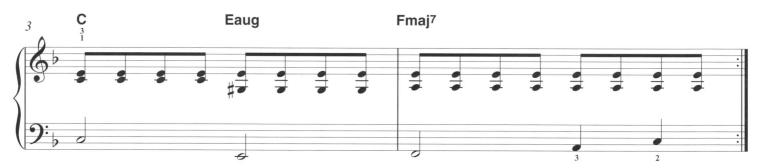

An - tho - ny works___ in the gro - cer - y store,___
Ser - geant O' Lear - y is walk - in' the beat,___ at

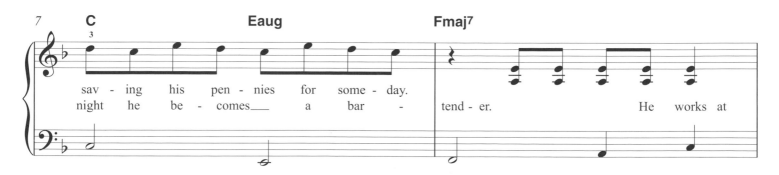

sav - ing his pen - nies for some - day.
night he be - comes___ a bar - tend - er. He works at

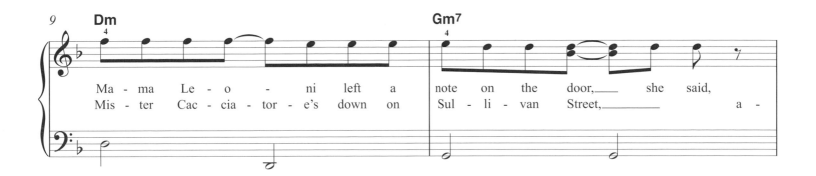

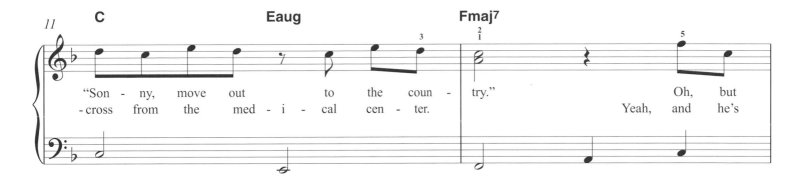

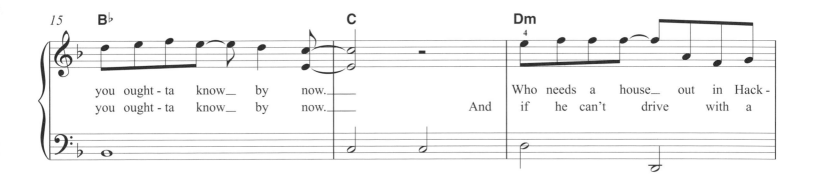

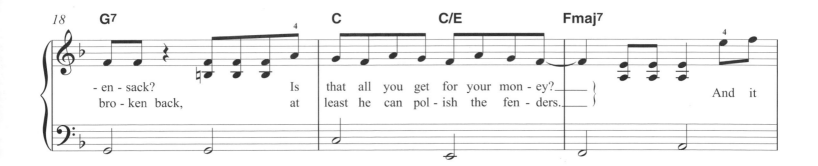

19

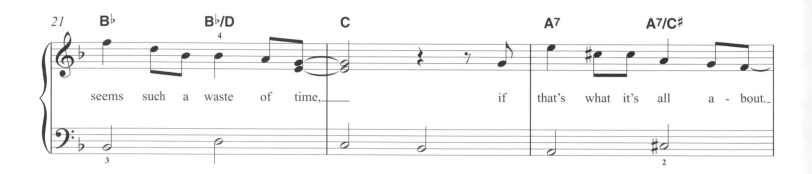

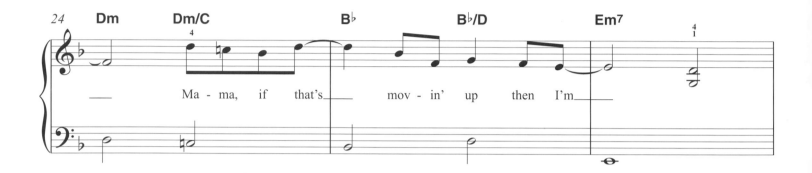

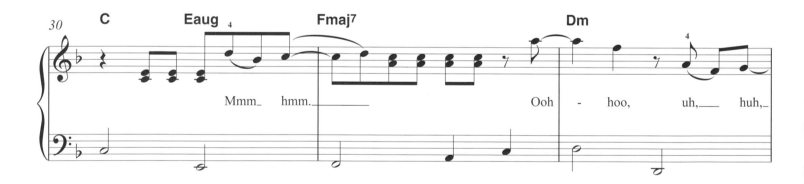

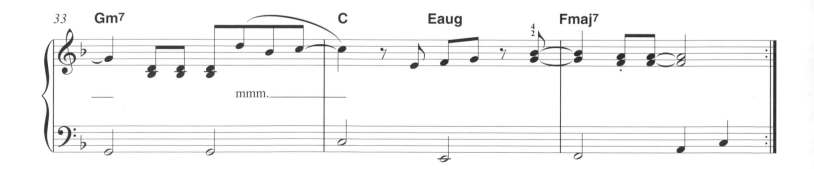

I'm___ mov - in' out.

My Life

Words and Music by Billy Joel

This song became the theme tune to the 1980 TV sitcom, *Bosom Buddies*, starring a young Tom Hanks. Due to licensing issues, it was not Joel's version of the song but a 'soundalike' that was created for the show. It was during the recording of this song that Joel's drummer, Liberty DeVitto, almost came to blows with producer Phil Ramone over the drum pattern, with DeVitto refusing to play in a disco style. Eventually, Ramone ordered DeVitto to do it his way and the song was a hit!

Hints & Tips: This song has a driving beat, and bars where the left hand has four crotchets/quarter notes really help to push the song along. You may, however, wish to try it slower than the marked tempo. Familiarise yourself with the structure of the song; there's a repeat and a D.S., so make sure you know your way round the score!

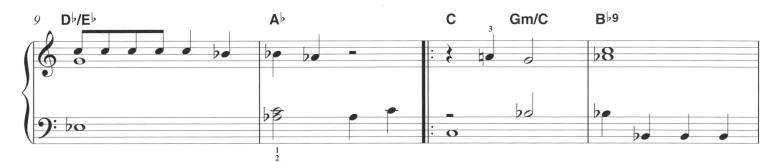

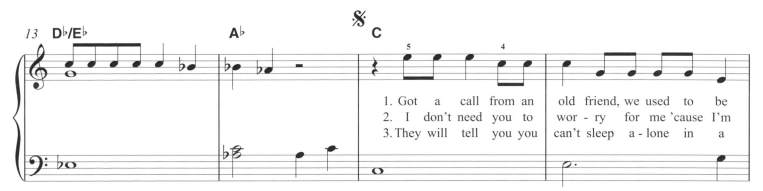

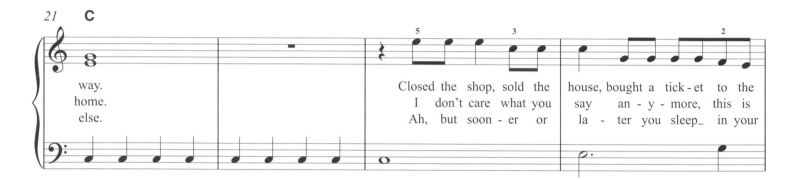

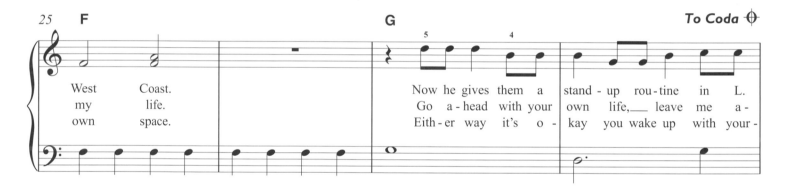

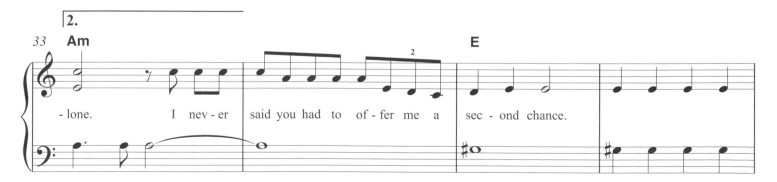

I nev-er said I was a vic-tim of cir-cum-stance.___

I still be - long. Don't get me wrong.

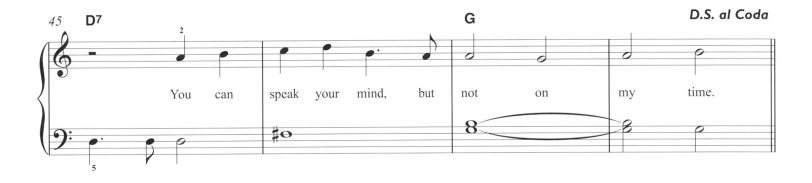

You can speak your mind, but not on my time.

D.S. al Coda

⊕ **Coda**

- self.

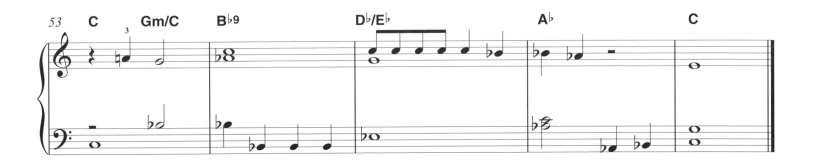

New York State of Mind

Words and Music by Billy Joel

Joel wrote this track en route back to New York on a Greyhound bus, having decided to move back to the city from California, finishing it on his arrival home. It appears on his fourth album, *Turnstiles*, released in 1976 and was covered by Barbra Streisand, Mel Tormé and Diane Schuur. The USA's beloved New York City has been celebrated by other artists, including Frank Sinatra with 'New York, New York' and Bruce Springsteen's 'New York City Serenade'.

Hints & Tips: Keep this song slow. This will enable you to really enjoy the bluesy chords. The vocal line is quite conversational in style, so don't worry too much about the rhythm.

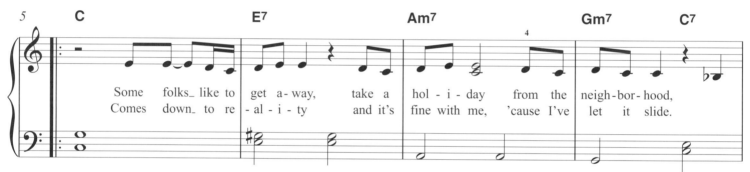

Some folks_ like to | get a-way, take a | hol-i-day from the | neigh-bor-hood,
Comes down_ to re | -al-i-ty and it's | fine with me, 'cause I've | let it slide.

hop a flight to | Mi-am-i Beach or to | Hol-ly-wood.
Don't care if it's | Chi-na-town or on | Riv-er-side.

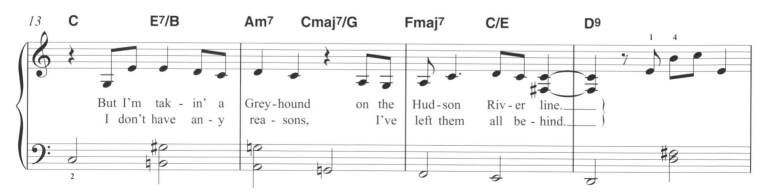

But I'm tak-in' a | Grey-hound on the | Hud-son Riv-er line.
I don't have an-y | rea-sons, I've | left them all be-hind.

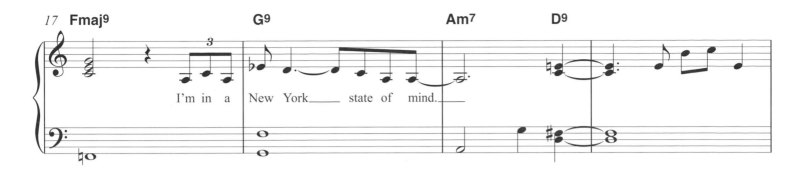

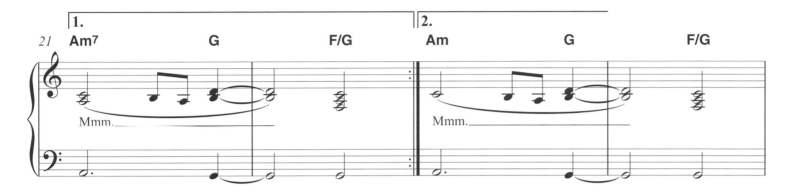

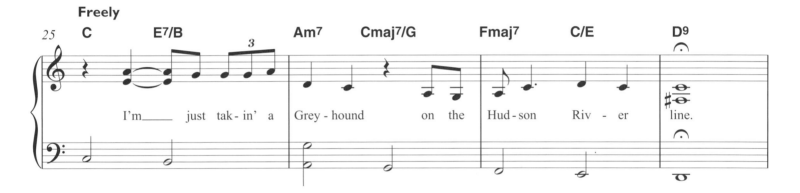

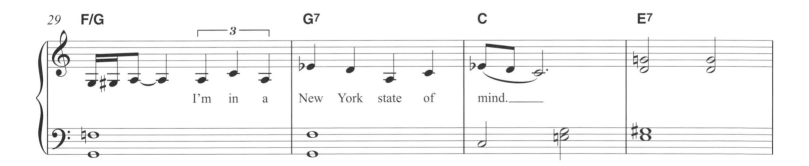

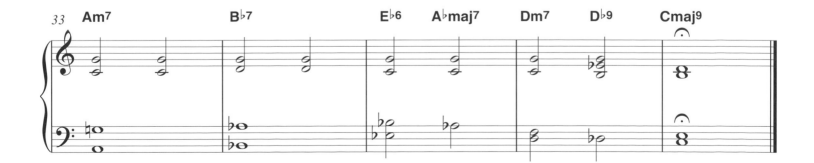

Only the Good Die Young

Words and Music by Billy Joel

This was quite the scandalous song to Catholic church officials when it was released in 1977! Church officials in America condemned the song, with one particular Catholic University banning the song from their radio station, which conversely stirred up publicity and track sales, making 'Only the Good Die Young' a massive hit! The track did so well that Joel later said in an interview, "I did write a letter to the archdiocese who'd banned it, asking them to ban my next record".

Hints & Tips: The intro to this song has a very different feel, because it has 'straight' quavers/eighth notes. When you get into the main part of the song, you need to feel the swing rhythm. Try this slowly at first. The left hand has quite a few chords that come in on the second beat. These can be played with a little more emphasis.

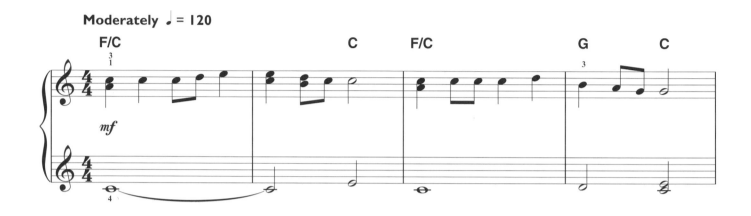

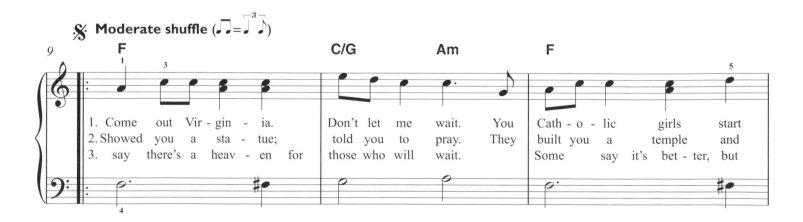

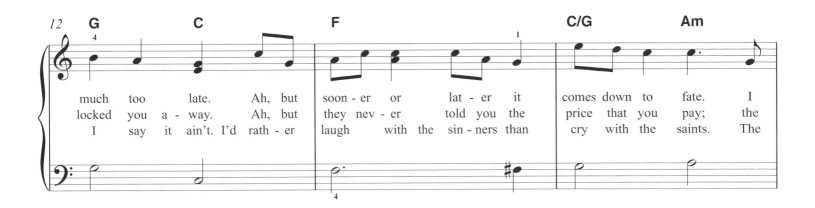

much too late. Ah, but
locked you a - way. Ah, but
I say it ain't. I'd rath - er

soon - er or lat - er it
they nev - er told you the
laugh with the sin - ners than

comes down to fate. I
price that you pay; the
cry with the saints. The

To Coda ⊕

1.

might as well be the
things that you might have
sin - ners are much more

one. Well, they

2.

done for

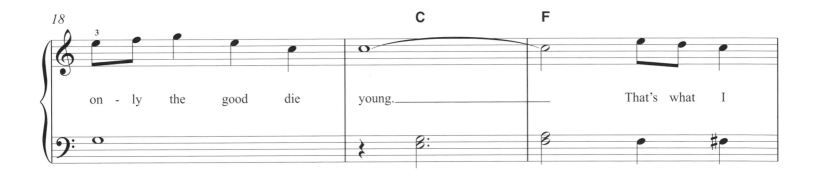

on - ly the good die

young.

That's what I

said.

On - ly the good die

young. On - ly the good die young.   You got a

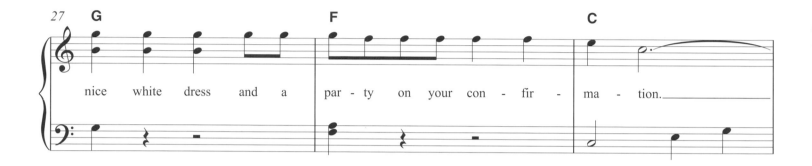

nice white dress and a   par - ty on your con - fir - ma - tion._____

_____ You've got a   brand new soul_____   and a   cross of gold._____

_____ But Vir - gin - ia, they did - n't give you   quite e - nough in - for -

-ma - tion._____   You did - n't   count on me

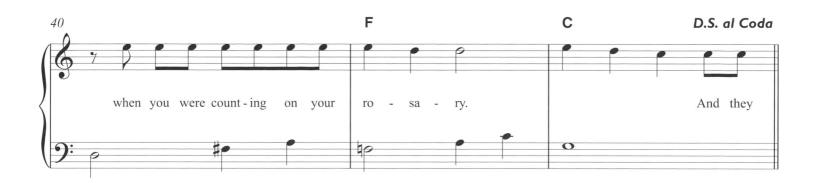

when you were count-ing on your ro - sa - ry. And they

Coda

fun. You know that on - ly the good die young.

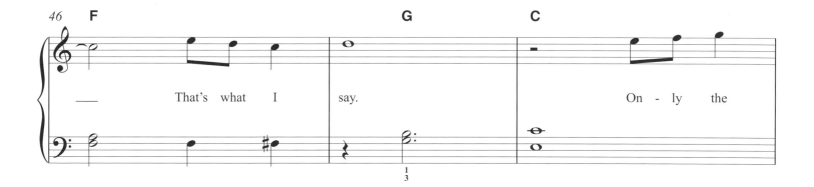

— That's what I say. On - ly the

good die young. On - ly the good die young.

Piano Man

Words and Music by Billy Joel

When his debut album, *Cold Spring Harbor*, didn't do too well in the charts in 1971, Joel was forced to find work and played for six months at The Executive Room piano bar in Los Angeles. During this time, Joel got to know the regulars and wrote 'Piano Man' about his time in the residency, including stories of real people he met at the venue. The Executive Room has since been demolished and a strip mall built in its place.

Hints & Tips: This song is in 'three', so it feels a bit like a pop waltz. The left hand can be reduced to just one note in most bars if you find that easier, although take care in places where the left hand needs to supply a melody note, e.g. in bars 16–17.

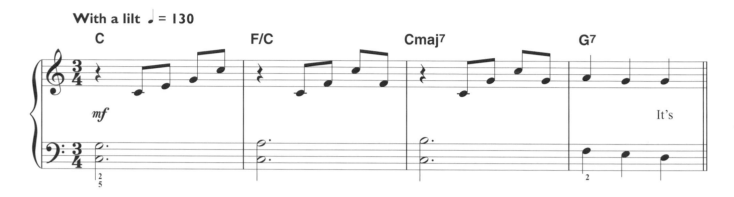

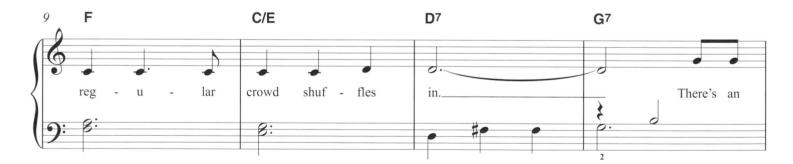

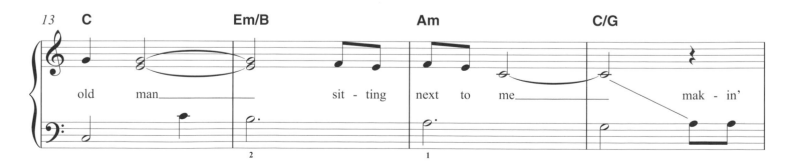

love to his ton - ic and gin.

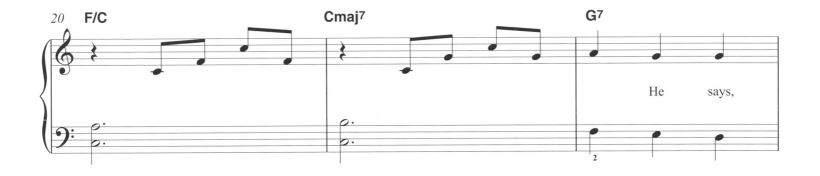

He says,

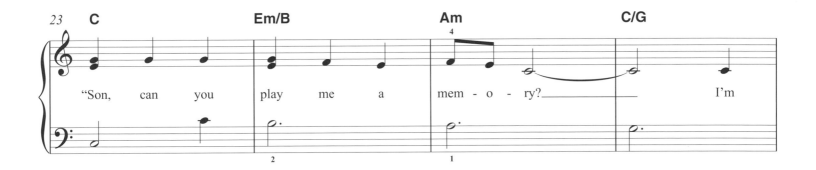

"Son, can you play me a mem - o - ry? I'm

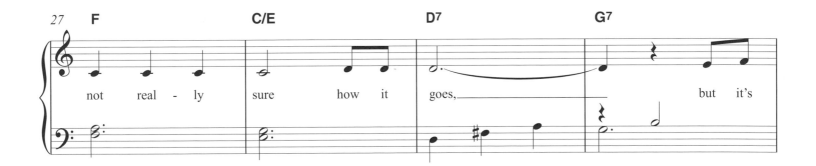

not real - ly sure how it goes, but it's

sad and it's sweet and I knew it com - plete when

33

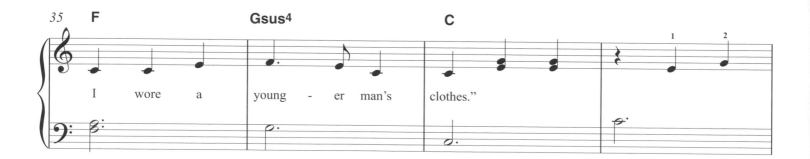

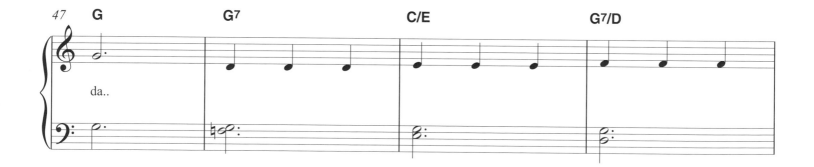

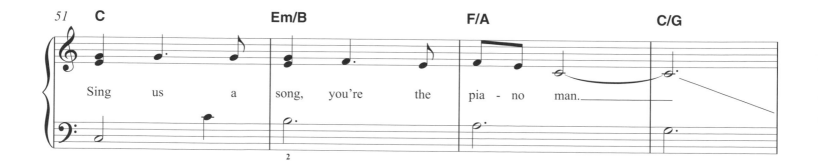

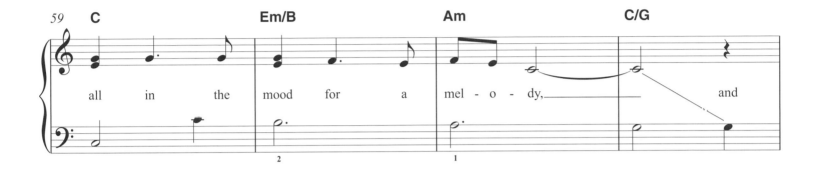

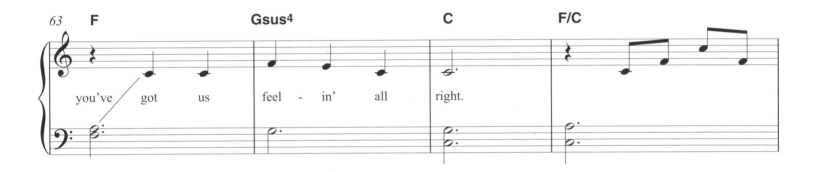

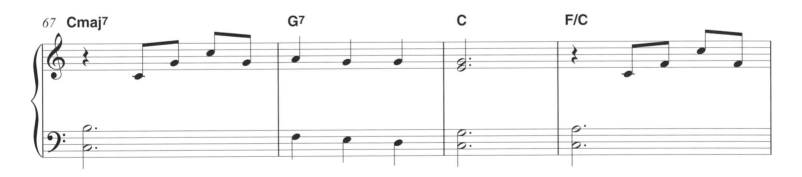

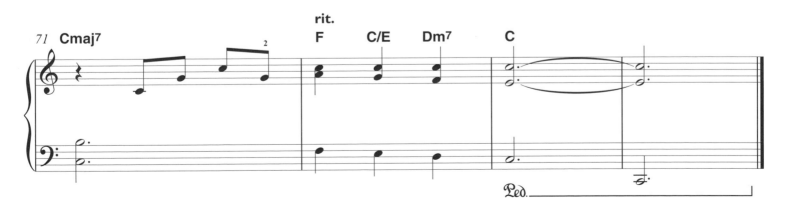

The River of Dreams

Words and Music by Billy Joel

Having admitted that a lot of his song inspirations come to him during dreams, Joel has always struggled to remember them upon waking. However, 'The River of Dreams' became an exception, with Joel remembering the song in great detail! The title is a play on the phrase 'stream of consciousness' and is in a gospel style, which Joel originally worried he wouldn't be able to pull off. The album of the same name was released in 1993, with cover art painted by Joel's then-wife, supermodel Christie Brinkley. Try to spot it on the cover of this book!

Hints & Tips: This song is in 2/2 which means two minims/half notes per bar. You can think of it as four crotchets/quarter notes instead if you prefer, but as you get to know it better you could speed it up a little. The gentle shuffle throughout the song helps propel the music forward.

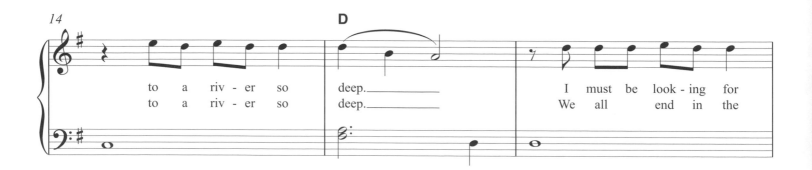

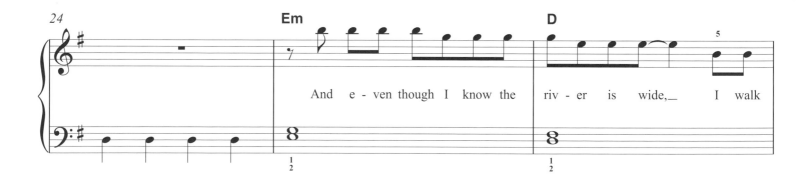

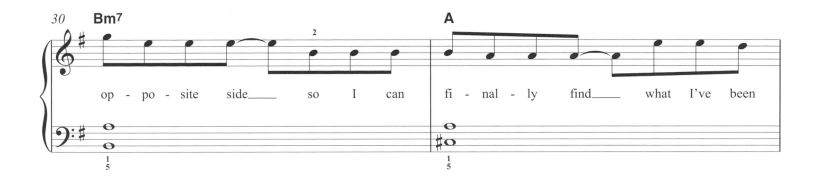

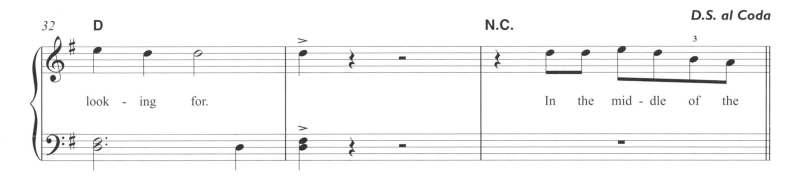

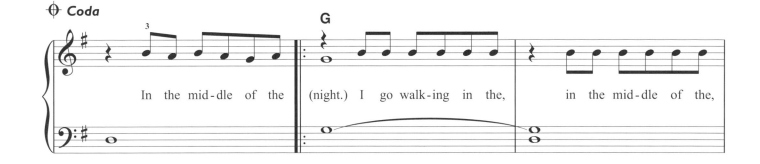

She's Always a Woman

Words and Music by Billy Joel

Joel's relationship with first wife, Elizabeth Weber, started out as an affair, as Weber was married to Joel's drummer at the time, Jon Small. After Small discovered the affair, Weber wasn't seen for several weeks, leaving Joel heartbroken, before her return to him and their consequent marriage. This song was written about Weber, who rallied against traditional gender roles of the time, becoming Joel's manager and working in a male-dominated industry with great success for a number of years.

Hints & Tips: Once you're comfortable with the notes of this song, you can take it a little faster, so it feels like 'one-in-a-bar'. Take care with the flats at the bottom of the third page. It feels quite far away from the home key at this point. Listening to the song would be a good idea.

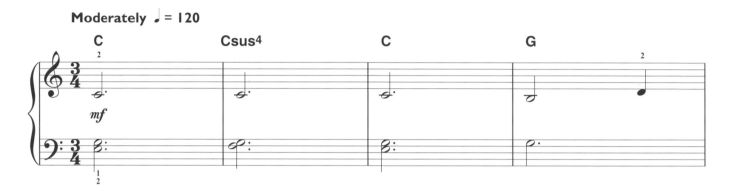

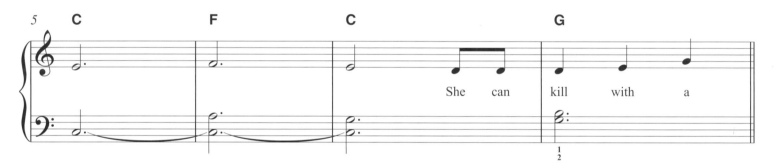

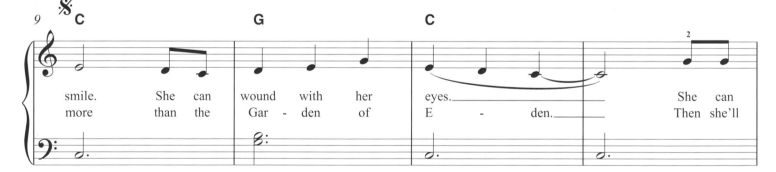

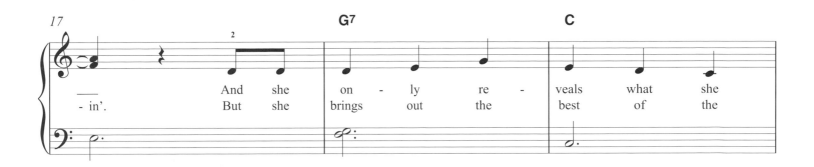

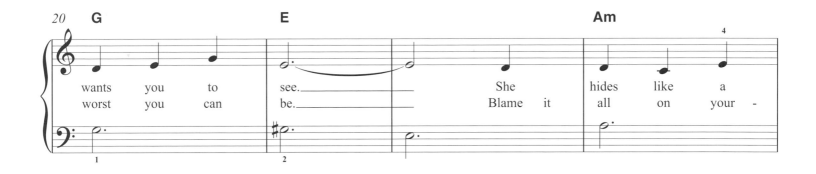

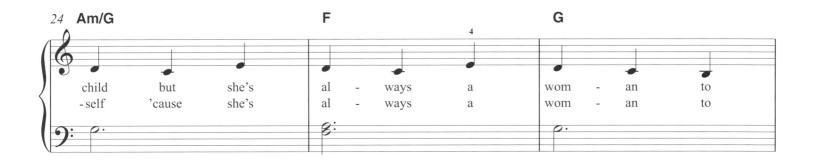

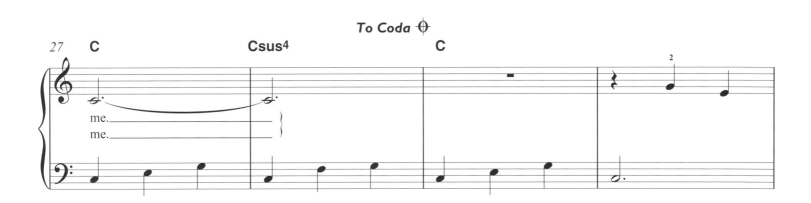

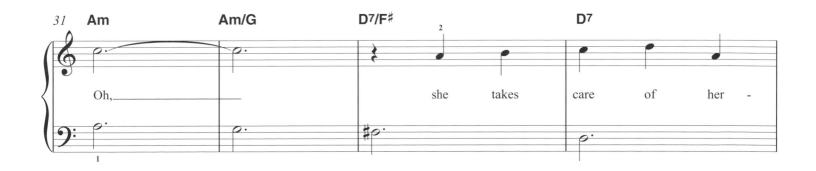

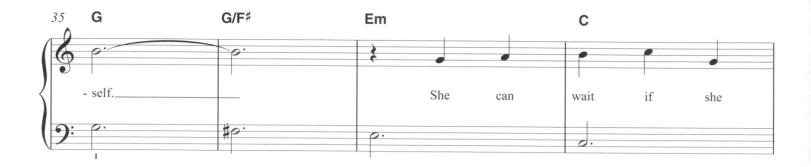

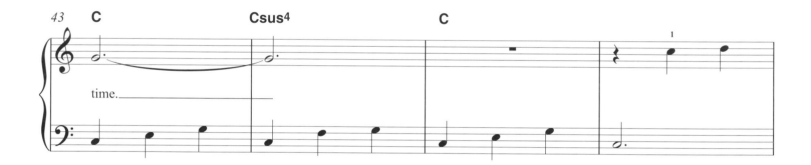

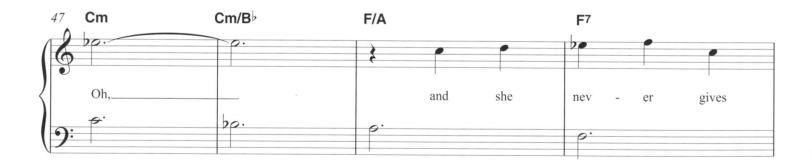

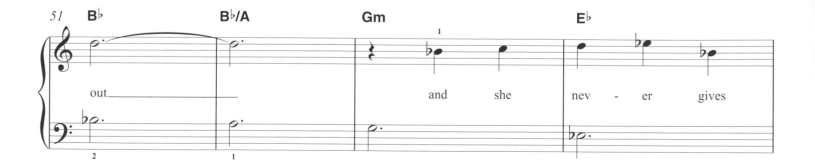

in,_____ she just chan - ges her

mind._____ And she'll prom - ise you

D.S. al Coda

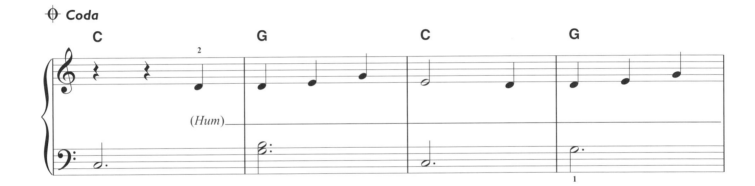

Coda

(Hum)_____

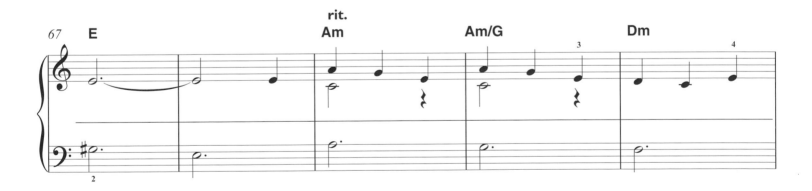

rit.

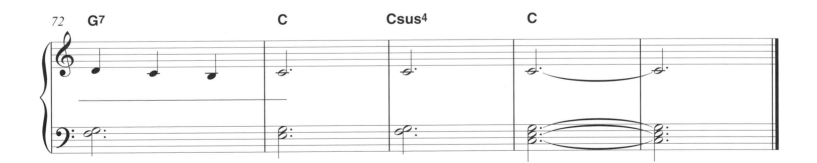

43

She's Got a Way

Words and Music by Billy Joel

Originally from his first album, *Cold Spring Harbor*, in 1971, Joel also included 'She's Got a Way' on his 1981 live album, *Songs in the Attic*. Another track from the debut record, 'Everybody Loves You Now', also made it to the live album, encouraging fans to revisit his older material. A connoisseur of writing about love, the song is said to be about first wife, Elizabeth Weber, whom he divorced in 1982.

Hints & Tips: The vocal line starts with a triplet, which is three even quavers/eighth notes across a beat. Try to keep this steady. The right-hand melody twists and turns a lot in the second page, negotiating its way through several changes of harmony. Keep your wrist relaxed so that it sounds gentle.

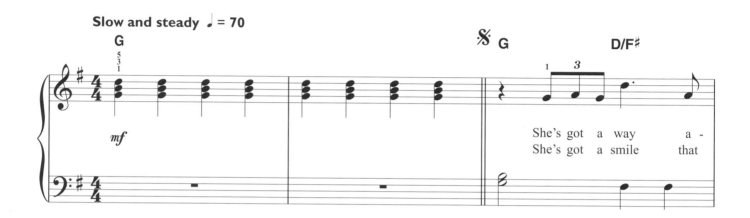

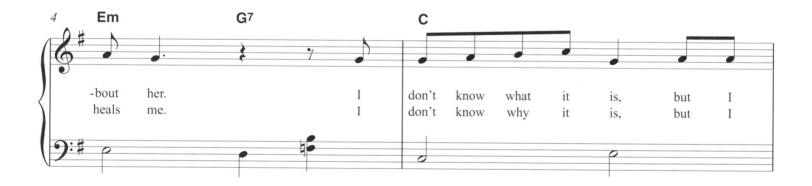

pleas - in'.
-bout her.
I
I
don't know why it is, but there
don't know what it is, but I

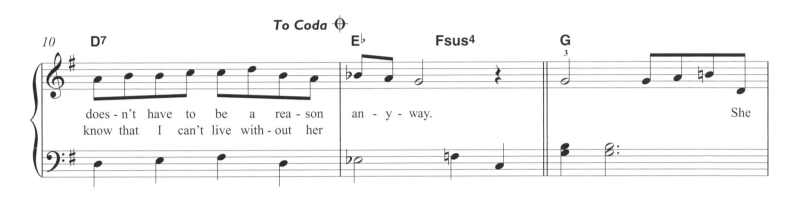

To Coda ⊕

does - n't have to be a rea - son
know that I can't live with - out her
an - y - way.

She

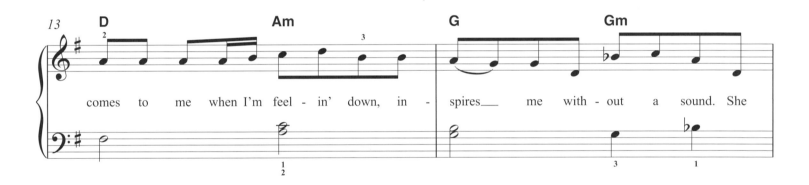

comes to me when I'm feel - in' down, in - spires___ me with - out a sound. She

D.S. al Coda

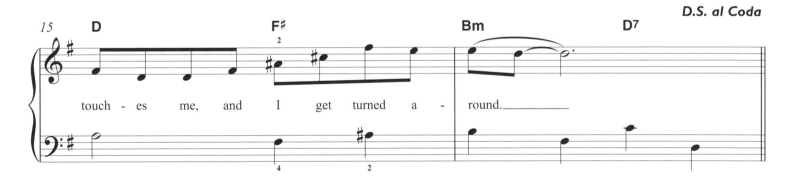

touch - es me, and I get turned a - round.___

⊕ Coda

rit.

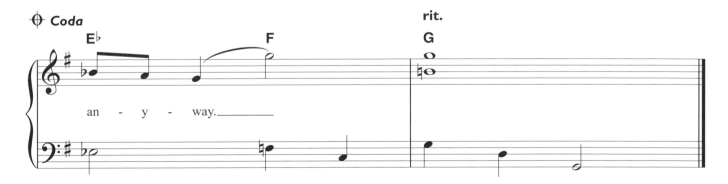

an - y - way.___

Uptown Girl

Words and Music by Billy Joel

This 1983 single earned Joel his first and only UK No. 1, which was later covered by Irish boyband Westlife in 2001 as part of BBC Comic Relief. The iconic music video features Joel as a car mechanic surrounded by his peers, attempting to woo the 'uptown girl' played by Christie Brinkley, whom Joel was married to from 1985 to 1994. Westlife paid tribute to the original video with their own version, portraying the five members working in a diner where they are visited by supermodel Claudia Schiffer.

Hints & Tips: This song has a heavy, driving beat, which helps move the music along.
You may wish to try a slower tempo, especially as you learn the notes in the second page.
Here, the harmony changes quite a bit and there are several flats and sharps to negotiate.

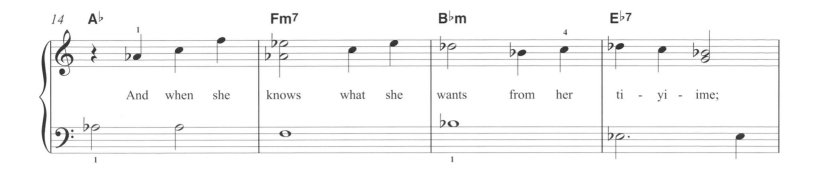

And when she knows what she wants from her ti - yi - ime;

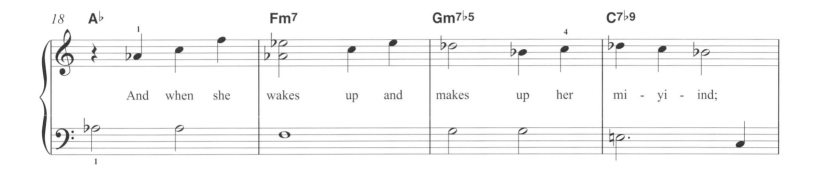

And when she wakes up and makes up her mi - yi - ind;

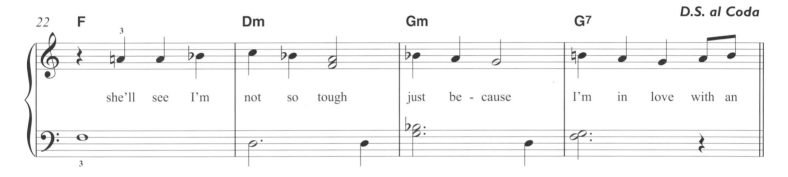

she'll see I'm not so tough just be - cause I'm in love with an

D.S. al Coda

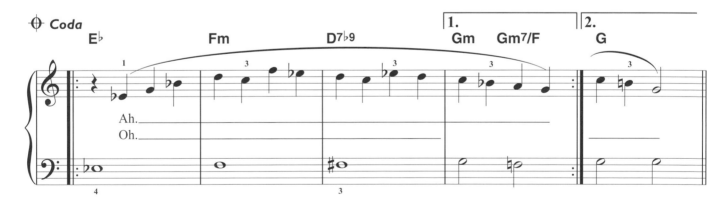

Coda

Ah.
Oh.

1.
2.

Up-town girl. She's my up-town girl. You know I'm in love with an Up-town girl.

Vienna

Words and Music by Billy Joel

Joel's father is at the forefront of this track, as Vienna was his father's birthplace and where he returned after divorcing Joel's mother to start a new family. It was used in the film *13 Going On 30* during a particularly nostalgic time for the main character, played by Jennifer Garner, when she returns to her childhood home. The song was so popular that when Joel would offer his audience a choice between 'Vienna' and another of his tracks, it often won out!

Hints & Tips: Have a listen to the song to get the sense of the slow swing. There are some big stretches in the right hand, e.g. the octave leap in bar 9. Play through the right hand on its own first. The left hand is much easier.

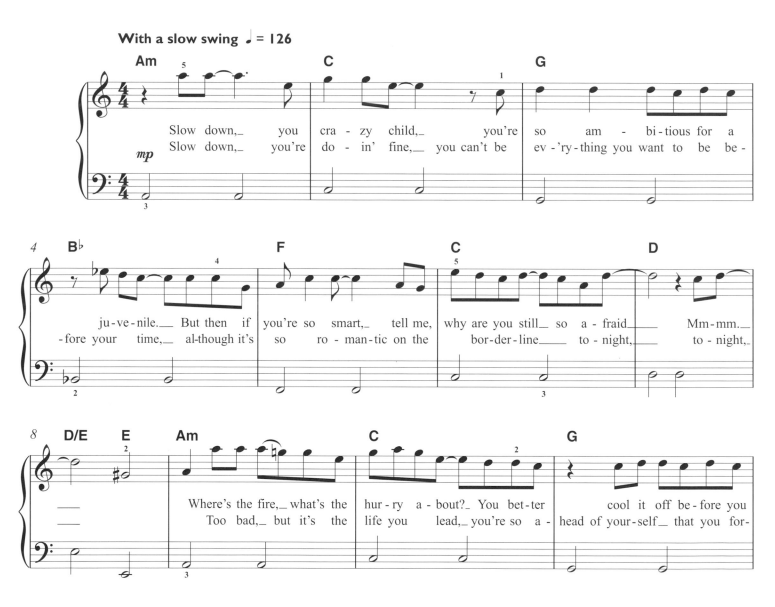

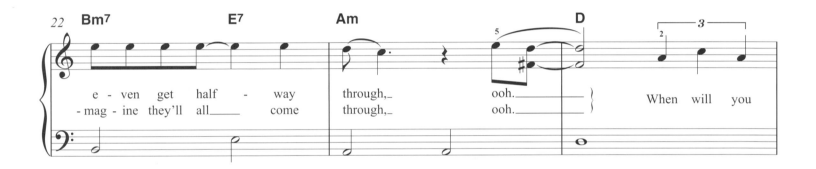

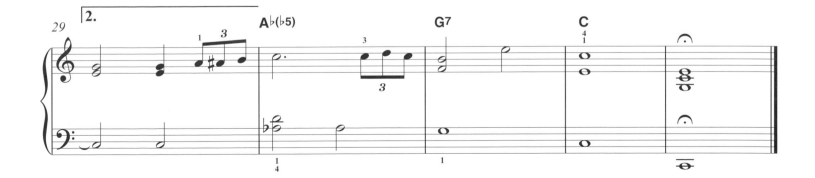

We Didn't Start the Fire

Words and Music by Billy Joel

The unrelenting lyrical style of this 1989 track was a different direction for Joel, reminiscent of R.E.M.'s 'It's the End of the World as We Know It (And I Feel Fine)' released two years before. Joel uncharacteristically started with just the lyrics after a conversation about the issues that his generation inherited as a result of major events caused by previous historical figures. When Joel performed this track live, he often sought cues from devoted audience members who knew the lyrics, as he found it difficult to recall them all!

Hints & Tips: Keep a relaxed wrist to play the right-hand repeated quavers/eighth notes evenly. The marked tempo is slower than the original, but as you get to know the notes better, you could speed things up a bit. Watch the F♯ in the key signature.

Ro - sen - bergs, H - Bomb, Sug - ar Ray, Pan - mun - jom, Bran - do, The King and I,

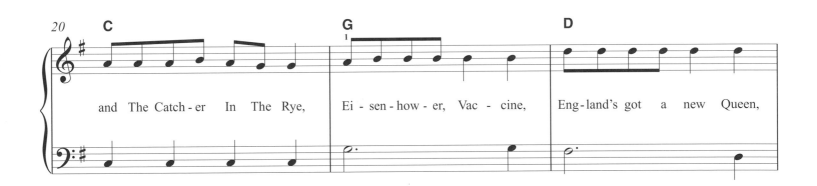

and The Catch - er In The Rye, Ei - sen - how - er, Vac - cine, Eng - land's got a new Queen,

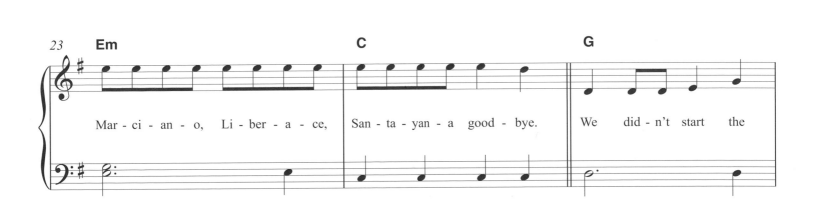

Mar - ci - an - o, Li - ber - a - ce, San - ta - yan - a good - bye. We did - n't start the

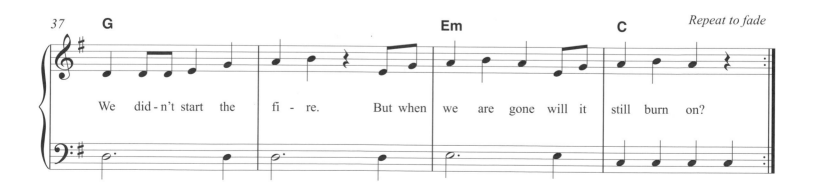

You May Be Right

Words and Music by Billy Joel

This is the first track from Joel's 1980 album, *Glass Houses*. Just before the track starts, the listener can hear shattered glass, which is a continuation of the album artwork of Joel about to throw a rock into a glass-walled house. It is a play on the phrase 'people who live in glass houses shouldn't throw stones', aimed at his critics. The song was used for the '90s TV show *Dave's World*, sung by Southside Johnny instead of the original track due to copyright issues.

Hints & Tips: Watch your 'F's in this song: there's an 'F♯' in the key signature but you actually play an 'F♮' in the main (guitar) theme at the beginning. Then when the vocal comes in, you go back to playing 'F♯'!

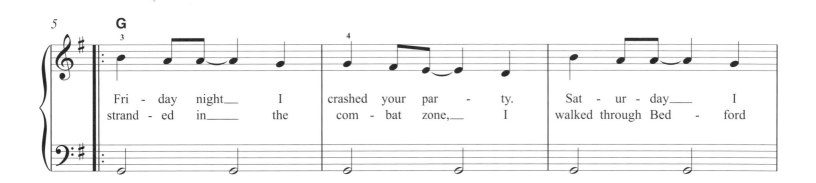

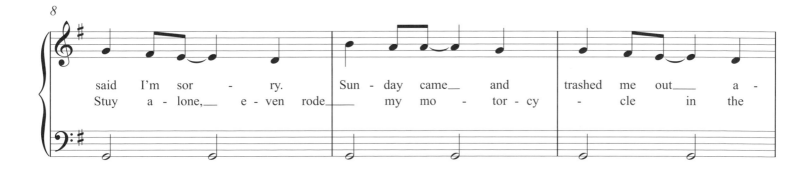

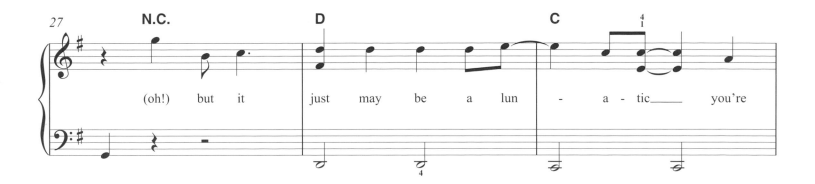

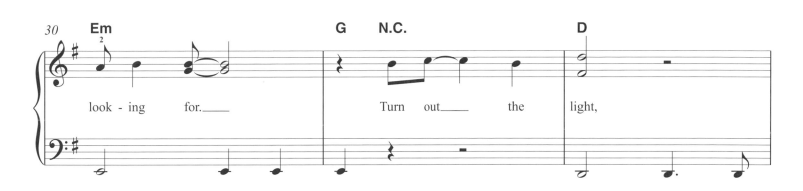

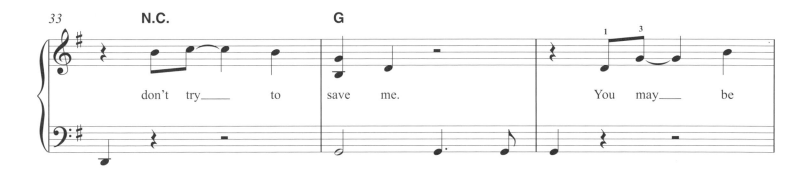